OUR RELATIONSHIP AND OUR WORK.

TO THE

INHABITANTS OF MUCH HOOLE AND LITTLE HOOLE,

FROM

THE REV. ROBERT BRICKEL,

RECTOR OF THE PARISH.

EASTER, 1864.

PRESTON:

PRINTED BY H. OAKEY, CAXTON HOUSE, FISHERGATE.

1864.

HOOLE,

EASTER, 1864.

———

MY DEAR PARISHIONERS,

There seems to be no need why I should write to you, when every Sabbath day I am preaching in our old Parish Church, and when any day I can have a welcome at your own fire sides; yet, having for some time thought that a few printed words from myself to you, about "OUR RELATIONSHIP AND OUR WORK," might be useful to us as a parish, I can delay no longer. Sickness has reminded me that what I think of doing had better be done at once.* May this written letter help us in our duty to God and one another, and remain for the furtherance of the Gospel.

I am the servant of God in the ministry of the Gospel, and your servant for Jesus Christ's sake.† At my admission into holy orders, nearly 30 years ago, I was asked by the Bishop, "Do you trust that you are inwardly moved by the Holy Ghost,—do you think that you are truly called, according to the will of our Lord Jesus Christ, and the due order of this realm, to the ministry of the Church, to serve God for the promoting of His glory and the edifying of His people?" My answers were, "I

* Ecclesiastes ix. 10.   † 2 Cor. iv. 5.

trust so—I think so." I had no doubt of it then, I have no doubt of it now; otherwise I should never have taken, or have continued to hold, the sacred office.* He who called me to the ministry, led me by his providence to this part of his vineyard; and I have now lived among you nearly 16 years, your servant for Jesus Christ's sake. Our relationship then is of God, whatever we may think, or however we may act. It is God who requires, that *you* should so account of us, as of the Ministers of Christ, and Stewards of the mysteries of God; and that *we* should be faithful to the ministry which we have received of Him, that we fulfil it.†

The Great Creator of all things hath been pleased, in this our world, to place men in very different positions and in very different circumstances; but with Him there is no respect of persons, and from all men He requires one and the same work, as the work of life. When the Jews said to Jesus Christ "What shall we do, that we may work the works of God?" He answered and said, "This is the work of God, that ye believe in Him whom He hath sent," ‡ And in the words of the aged Apostle, this is the commandment of God, "That we should believe in the name of His Son Jesus Christ and love one another." § Now a right faith, not the

* Ezekiel xiii. 3.   † 1 Cor. iv. 1, 2 ; Col. iv. 17.   ‡ John vi. 28.   § 1 John iii. 23.

faith which a man may say he has, but a right faith in Jesus Christ, will make a man, whatever his position, or whatever his circumstances, a man of God, seeking to do his *best* in every relationship of life, at home and in the world—and in every part of his calling, at the loom or in the fields.*

Even so—the work of God required from those appointed to the ministry is, that we know nothing among you but Christ and Him crucified;† but in a right knowledge of this, we have our own eternal life; ‡ and are made, in every good thing, whether temporal or eternal, whether for this world or the next, the willing servants of those amongst whom we have to labour.

Such then is our relationship, and such our work: and I am writing this letter, in the hope and with the prayer, that we may be furthered in fulfilling the duties of that relationship, and in performing the different parts of that work. Our subject then will have to be things temporal and things eternal (for true religion includes *both)*— what has been done, and what remains to be done.

I. We will begin with things temporal. I am thankful to say, that when we consider what *has been*, and what *is,* in the external habits and

* James ii. 26.   † 1 Cor. ii. 2.   ‡ John xvii. 31.

circumstances of our parish, we may take courage and have a good hope for the future.

1. *The time was* when nearly all our young men and women were dependent upon that pauperizing machine, the hand-loom. The sound of the shuttle, though cheerful in itself, was to me most saddening, associated as it was with bad wages, uncertain employment and a poor prospect; but I thank God, that as in other places, so in Hoole at last, our young people have given up the hand-loom, and have found better wages with the power-looms at Walmer Bridge. May God preserve them from one great temptation connected more especially with this kind of work; the temptation to leave home and board elsewhere, that they may keep or spend their own wages without the control of father and mother: but woe to those who, in the desperate wickedness of their hearts, thus abuse God's providence, and prove themselves to be without natural affection.* For the change of work, however, we have reason to be thankful. By the hand-loom men cannot live; by the power-loom they may. There are, however, some who, by peculiar circumstances, are bound to the hand-loom probably for life; and there will always be many in Hoole who, though having children at the mill, can yet

* Proverbs xxx. 17.

find no work for themselves. For such as these, when without work, or waiting for work, the cultivation of a large garden would be a help and a comfort in many ways; and this system (usually called the Allotment system) was favorably regarded as a likely means of helping ourselves when we were compelled to have help from the Relief-fund. I shall, at any time, be very glad to speak to the landowners, in behalf of those who are disposed to act upon it. And now, whilst thanking God for better wages and better work, and praying that through His providence these may never fail, but continue to improve; I must also, in your name and for myself, thank the firm at Walmer Bridge, that their mill was kept open when so many others were shut up.

2. *The time was* when the young men of the parish—from the Marsh, the Moss, and Hoole town—herding together in gangs, and assembling at the idle Corners, fought with each other from time to time, and regularly insulted the passers by, more especially the women; but now, as a body, our young men, and even the lesser lads, consider these things mean, disgraceful, cowardly, and altogether beneath them, whilst the number of the base and ill-mannered ones is continually decreasing. Instead, therefore, of the remark which I have heard,

that there was no place, between Preston and Liverpool, so given to coarseness and the abuse of travellers, as our own neighbourhood; it can now be truly said, that in few places are the young men quieter and better behaved.* The young ought to have amusement and recreation; and as a parish we have striven to afford something of this kind by our yearly feasts—the school feast at midsummer, the harvest home in autumn, the concert and tea-party at Christmas; and let every one of us, old and young, masters and servants, take his part at these social gatherings. A village band, such as the one so creditably raised and conducted at Walmer Bridge, does good service in raising young men above the vulgar amusements of idle corners and coarse insults to women and strangers. For winter evenings, we have the night school and library. For summer, in addition to your gardens and cucumber beds, and a quiet stroll to the Marsh, there might perhaps be a cricket club; as the Devil is sure to find mischievous and wicked work for idle hands. And that the savings of our young men may not be changed into "fools' pence," we hope, when better times come, to have a House and Stock club; that from wages laid up, they may furnish a house, or stock a small farm. By the *Post Office* Savings' Bank and Insurance

* 1 Peter iii. 8.

Office, *Government* offers a helping hand to the provident; and I think that when the young man goes to the Savings Bank, the husband and father should apply to the Insurance Office, of *Government:* these cannot fail. One or two hundred pounds would, with God's blessing, be a help to the widow and children in carrying on the Farm; and when such a sum can be secured (through Government) to the family at his death, by the payment of a few pounds yearly, some such provision ought to be made by the husband and father; but the men, who in their youth have had their standing place at the idle corners, are generally speaking not the men for either Savings Banks or Insurance Offices. May the idle corners of the parish be *wholly* abolished.

3. *The time was* when the parish, and more especially Hoole town, abounded in nasty stagnant ditches, whence issued sickness and death. These and many other bodily ills will come in spite of every precaution. Any of these we may have to endure at any time if God sees fit thus to try us; but, for a man to have a filthy ditch before his door, or by the way side, poisoning the good air which God has given us, is a wrong both to himself and his neighbour. In your persons and your houses, few parishes exceed Hoole as regards cleanliness;

and to this I attribute, under God, much of the freedom from those evils, which always attend filthy ditches and bad watercourses; but *I know for a fact*, that, from these very things, some of our neighbours have suffered severe sickness, and others have been hurried to the grave. If a man had a right (which he has not) to keep a nuisance on his own premises, and to breed fevers for himself and his family, he has no right thus to injure his neighbour. We rejoice, then, that many very large ditches before our cottages have been filled up, and that a considerable length of bad watercourses by the wayside has been properly drained. In Hoole town, where nearly every cottage had its own ditch before its own door, there are now, in the place of ditches, gardens with fruits and flowers; a little more improvement would make it what every English village ought to be.

4. As in these, so in the much greater evils of drunkenness and bastardy, there has been a manifest decrease. With respect to the former, we have had a lesson, which I pray may never be forgotten. At one time, much of Hoole was in easily rented tenements or occupied by the owners, whilst the weaver, instead of the 3s. he is now receiving, had 30s. for the same piece of work; prosperity was flowing in upon the parish, but the gain was made a

a loss; the blessing was changed into a curse by *the bottle and the glass.* The land became impoverished, for the tenants never thought of manuring, nor the owners of draining. Families of farmers, once well to do, and of weavers receiving large wages, became wretchedly poor; but though the like profits will never be realised again by either one or the other, yet as there is better management by the farmer, and greater thriftiness by the cottager, with less drunkenness in both Farmer and Cottager, we are as a parish much quieter and somewhat richer.

The time was when for the 3,000 acres in Hoole, not a single acre was Tile-drained, nor scarcely a ton of Manure purchased; but now, by the occupiers as a class, we have good manuring, and by the owners much more draining; five percent being paid thereon by the farmer, less than which no wise tenant will grudge, and more than which no just land-owner will expect. And it is very likely that our improved cultivation of late will be much exceeded in the next few years. A recent change of ownership has already led to great results, in both manure and drains. Our farm houses, and outbuildings with *tanks,* are also now better attended to. The additions and alterations just completed on the estate belonging to

J. Dauntesey, Esq., are as convenient and comfort-
able as the most improving farmer could desire; and
other proprietors are helping their tenants in the
same way.

Farmers, and especially the farmers of Hoole,
with heavier poor rates than usual, on account of the
cotton famine, need help; and in the cultivation of
the land help will be given, by every just proprietor,
to those tenants deserving of encouragement. The
extra burden, laid upon us by our union with Preston in poor law matters, may be known by the fact,
that last year the poor of Little Hoole, not in-
cluding those upon the common fund elsewhere,*
were relieved for £26, whilst the poor rates
paid and borrowed by the township amounted to
£452. A small sum would have to be apportioned
to the township for other necessary charges. But the
disproportion is caused chiefly by the circumstance,
that the irremovable poor (always a goodly number in a manufacturing town) are now chargeable,
not to the township in which they have been work-
ing, but to the *Union* at large.

Our present farmers, however, are striving, care-
ful, and temperate; and I hope that, by the blessing
of God upon their labours, they may be able, not-
withstanding the present high rates and little

* One family, I know, has been thus relieved.

profits, to pay every man his due, providing things honest in the sight of all men, ever having a sufficiency for themselves, and something to spare for those in need. When any of you are pressed for money, and should have to sell at a disadvantage to make your payments, if the postponement of my tithe rent for 6, 12, or 18 months, would be of any use, I should be very glad to give such further delay *whenever you apply*.

Before leaving this part of our subject, I ought perhaps to notice an objection which may have arisen in the minds of some, " What has our Clergyman to do with the farming of the parish, or the filling up of ditches ?" Many years ago, a young man, when rebuked for his shameful and wicked conduct to a young woman, answered me by asking, " What had I to do with it ?" And to my question, " What do you suppose I am in the parish for ?" gave me the reply, " To marry and to bury folks." You would *all* however expect me to do something more than this. It is indeed true, that because our parish is cut up into small parcels, and from our having no great landed proprietor resident, I have had more to do with temporal things, than I like: but as I have already said, religion consists not merely in preaching and praying, and attending public worship and the sacraments ; these things *must* be done as means of grace : but if your religion does not make you *better men* in *every* respect—better as husbands and fathers, children and brothers; better as farmers, and weavers, and labourers, it is not worth much; and if my office does not lead me to be interested in your improvement of temporal things, and to rejoice and wish you God speed, I am not regarding you as I ought. But I thank God for you, that there is better farming and less drunkenness in the parish than in times past.

5. As regards fornication and bastardy—these great evils were scarcely less common than drunkenness; when a woman could have half a dozen illegitimate children; when a man and woman unmarried could live together as husband and wife, or, living in different families, could live in habitual fornication; when a man could have his one, two, or three bastards by different women; when such things could be, and the guilty ones go in and out among us without shame, visiting and being visited by respectable people, the morality of the parish was becoming very like that of Sodom and Gomorrah. I thank God that the worst of these things have altogether passed away, and though some of them are not unknown even now, yet that by the parish at large all such are considered disgraceful and wicked, and not merely misfortunes

and things of course, as in times past. Now and then, perhaps, there may be found a young woman who is rather the seducer than the seduced; yet our young women, as a class, are very anxious to keep themselves pure in this matter before God and man; and I beseech you, *young men*, for the sake of your own mothers and sisters, your future wives and daughters, to flee fornication: for their sakes, as well as for your own, when youthful lusts are strong, and the Devil is helping you to an opportunity, lift up your hearts in prayer that you may be kept, by the power of God, from such great wickedness. Even they, who indulge these lusts, feel in their hearts that they cannot respect the woman whom they have seduced, as they would have done if she had kept her honour; whilst all men, except the most degraded, burn with anger at any such wrong done to the women of their own family. How can you then trample on the modesty of those whom you profess to love, and break down the barrier which God has given them as their glory, and thus lead other men, by *your example*, to inflict this the greatest possible injury upon your own children? If you will do these things, be sure your sin will find you out, even in this world. Marriage is honourable in all, and the bed undefiled; but whoremongers and adulterers God will judge. Have your courtships, but let not your following be that of brute beasts. Can parents have anything to answer for in this matter? It may be so; for when the sons of Eli made themselves vile, and the father restrained them not, he was held accountable to a certain extent and punished. We know indeed that parents cannot give grace to their children; and that the son, when grown up, is sometimes too stiffnecked for discipline, especially if he has not been firmly, and lovingly, and prayerfully trained; still there might be, and there always should be—what there very frequently is not—the severe rebuke for the wickedness of fornication. Besides, when the children are young, do not many parents unthinkingly injure them, by having boys and girls, 10 or 12 years old, in the same sleeping apartment with themselves or with each other? I am aware that many cottages have wretched accommodation; but in this, as in other things, we are moving, though slowly, in the right direction, and the owners of such property are seeing it to be their duty that no house shall have fewer than three sleeping rooms, when the number of the family requires it.

Brethren, I thank God, that there has been a change for the better in these things; that the hand-loom has been succeeded by the power-loom; that our stagnant ditches have been filled up; that our manners are less rude and more civilized; that we have our land better drained and manured; and that there is a great decrease in drunkenness and bastardy. And now, in the name of God, I call upon the parish to be true to itself, and never to allow any filthiness in manner, speech, or deeds to prevail as in times past; that there may be no going back; that the old proverb of " The dog returning to his vomit, and the sow to her wallowing in the mire," may never be applied to us; for then, our last state would be worse than the first. There are now, and there probably always will be, a few who would rather have a ditch than a garden, rudeness instead of civility—drunkenness instead of temperance—bastardy instead of a married life; but they are in a great minority, and, God helping us, we will keep them so, praying that they may be ashamed of themselves before it be too late.

By such as these—who hate reformation of any kind, either in themselves or their neighbours, and by some others, probably for other reasons—I have been slandered and misrepresented, from time to time, in my ministerial work. I am sorry that they who bear false witness, or who so readily receive it when borne by others, against their Minister and their neighbours, should continue to inflict so great an injury upon themselves for the next world, by doing the Devil's work in this. But the words spoken against me, I forgive. "It is enough for the disciple that he be as his master, and the servant as his Lord."

6. A great help, in keeping us from going back, will be our schools. You remember the place we used to have for the education of the young, then part of a weaver's cottage, at present a shippon. In such a building, no teacher could work with any credit to himself or profit to his scholars; but now, we have lofty, many-windowed, and well-aired National Schools; and I shall never forget how that for the erection of these, the farmers carted the materials, whilst the poor hand-loom weavers came, on Saturdays and Mondays, with spade, pick-axe, and barrow to assist in the excavations. These schools, with others at Walmer Bridge, erected by Messrs. Mc.Kean & Co., entirely at their own expense, are being carried on in full efficiency; and, in your name and for myself, I thank the trustees of both schools for their help in this good work. When thus assisted in the education of your children, there will, I hope and pray, be no likelihood of a return to the bad manners and habits of former times.

Speaking of things done by us in our relationship, as Minister and people, I am glad in being able to say that—as in the erection of schools—so in the beautifying and enlargement of our old Church—the extension of God's Acre—the purchase of a clock "In memoriam Horroccii," &c., &c.—we have acted together as a parish, for good and against evil. You have given cheerfully in helping forwards these and other material improvements, which have cost altogether about £1200, as recorded in the vestry book of charities; and, regarding any additional outlay, you, as well as myself, would have been very ready to rest and be thankful; but, the parish having had to suffer from time to time from the non-residence of the Clergyman, because there was no house attached to the Church; and the Manor House, usually occupied by the Clergyman, being two miles from the Church and schools; it has been thought desirable to build a Rectory; and an account is opened by trustees with the Preston Banking Company for that purpose. I thank Sir Thomas G. Hesketh for the site; the patron, land-owners, and personal friends for their subscriptions; and I thank my parishioners for the good and willing offer to cart the materials.

II. These changes for the better have not been effected without labour and selfdenial; yet these things may be done, and much greater improvement take place—and we all know there is room—whilst the "majora," as our Horrocks has it, the greater, the mightier things, the things eternal, may be left undone, and then what would it profit? Nay, what would it profit, if a man should gain the whole world and lose his own soul?*

Religion indeed requires that a man should make the best use of his talents,† and so leave the hand-loom for more remunerative employment, if he can find such; that he should follow his calling, whether it be to rule a kingdom or sweep a street, in the best possible manner;‡ that he should not be ill-mannered, but courteous;§ that he should not injure himself or his neighbour by poisoning God's pure air with stagnant ditches; that he should not be either a drunkard or a fornicator; ‖ and that Churches and schools should be suitably kept.¶ But though no man can be thoroughly doing the will of God who does not thus act in *every thing* according to the ability which God may give him, still, if his righteousness is nothing more than this, he is yet very far from the kingdom of God, and can have no true religion.

Hitherto I have been speaking of Hoole as a parish. The Church is yours, the schools are yours. As a parish you enlarged and beautified the Church

---

* Matt. xvi. 26,   † Matt. xxv. 14.   ‡ Prov. xii. 11.   § 1 Pet. iii. 8.
‖ 1 Cor. vi. 10.   ¶ Haggai i. 14.

and built the schools; and as a parish we have given up some of our bad habits, and have adopted better ones; but now, I want *every man* to look into his own heart and reflect upon his own life. The message of God, which I am commissioned to declare, is to each man individually. Of the truth of that message, there cannot be the shadow of a doubt, for it is the Truth of God. We speak what we know; and, being fully assured of the certainty of those things which we believe,* we have declared them unto you, that ye also may have fellowship with us; and truly our fellowship is with the Father and with His Son Jesus Christ.†

1. Our message is the Truth of God, for God Himself hath spoken unto us. That the Bible is the Word of God; that holy men of old spake as they were moved by the Holy Ghost; that all Scripture is given by inspiration of God—we all profess to believe; and though, if Christians indeed, we have a witness in our hearts that these things are so, and are ourselves an epistle of God;‡ still, it is good for us, in these times especially, to consider *why* we believe that the Bible is the Word of God, and that God Himself speaketh unto us in the Old and New Testament. One reason for our doing so, is that the Bible contains 66 books,

* Luke i. 4.   † 1 John i. 3.   ‡ 2 Cor. iii. 3.

penned by about 30 writers, within the period of 1600 years. That so many books—written at sundry times so widely distant—by men so very differently circumstanced—and about things not to be discovered by human wisdom—should, whilst entirely distinct, be yet so mutually dependent, and so explanatory of each other, as to make *one* book, with *one* grand subject, and *one* great purpose, with some apparent, but without a single real contradiction, is a thing utterly impossible, except under the superintendence of *one mind*, which could *only* be the mind of God. The Bible, therefore, being written according to the mind of God, is the word of God. "It has God for its author, salvation for its end, and truth, without any mixture of error, for its matter." There are many other proofs, such as :—Secondly, The miracles wrought.—Thirdly, The prophecies uttered by many of the writers.—Fourthly, The present state of the Jewish nation, which is both a miracle and a fulfilment of prophecy.—Fifthly, The subject of the Revelation so fitting in with man's necessities, &c., &c. There is also another fact which, *of itself alone*, proves undoubtedly that Christianity is from and God, that the Bible is the Word of God. By His resurrection from the dead, of which thing, as an historical fact, there is better evidence than for any other in the world, Jesus Christ proved himself to be the Truth. Now the Old Testament was always appealed to by our Saviour as the Word of God; and the New Testament was written by those, to whom He gave the Holy Ghost for that very purpose. Therefore we believe, upon the testimony of Jesus Christ, that God hath spoken unto us; and that He commanded his word to be written, in time past unto the fathers by the prophets, and in these last days unto us, by certain witnesses chosen by the Son of God to declare what they had seen and heard;* that believing in God and His Christ revealed in the Scriptures of Truth, we might have life everlasting.

2. God hath spoken unto us, and as the servant of God, and your servant in Jesus Christ, I have a message from God to *each one* of you.† In declaring that message, I will not speak to you of things about which some in the parish may differ from me; how that the Nation, as such, should render national homage to the Almighty by a National Church founded on the Word of God; how that in the Christian Church there ought to be the three orders of Bishops, Priests, and Deacons; and how that, in the public worship of God, it is desirable to have a Liturgy. Of these and some other things, though fully persuaded in my own mind, others may entertain different opinions:

---

* 1 John i. 3.   † Ezekiel iii. 17.

and they ought to have, what I claim for myself, full liberty of thought and action. If we cannot be of one mind, we should agree to differ; if we cannot have uniformity, we should have, as far as we can, unity of spirit. I and others are of the Church of England; some may prefer to differ from it in different ways; and such differences will needs be, arising from a variety of causes; but let us guard against murmurings, and disputings, and endless divisions;* for though such things are natural, yet God is a God, not of confusion, but of order; and for our opinions and practices in *this*, as in all other things, we must account to Him. Before, however, we proceed to things more important, about which there is no difference among Christians, I must very briefly touch upon another question, the vexed question of Church Rates. There can be no doubt whatever that the law requires, and, if they refuse, would compel the parishioners to keep the Parish Church in repair, and to provide things necessary for the decent performance of Divine Service. The *amount* of the rate, whether it should be less or more, *may* be disputed; but the *principle* of the rate *cannot* be legally questioned. There have been Church Rate abuses in this parish as elsewhere, for the ratepayers themseves would have it so; but at present, our Church Rates are only

---

* Romans xvi. 17.

half of what they used to be; and I hope I am not too confident in saying that, perhaps with scarcely an exception, the whole of the parish will give the Wardens and myself credit for desiring to lessen the amount, whenever it is possible; and for requiring nothing whatever that is really contrary to law. The principle we can never give up, and the law has established it; but, in the amount expended, there shall be the greatest economy. There has been a little grumbling (as was natural), but hitherto we have had no open quarrelling or litigation; and I am thankful to those who, though opposed to Church Rates, have not disturbed the peace of the parish in this matter; but have given us credit for doing what we can, according to the present law. If, however, any tenant ratepayer should be determined in refusing payment of his Church Rates, I would willingly help the wardens to try and beg it of the landowner, before they proceeded to extremities; for the beginning of strife is like the letting out of water.*

3. Passing by these and other such questions, let me now delare to you plainly, yet briefly, the message of God, which must be received and obeyed by *every one that* would enter into the kingdom of heaven. God hath spoken to us,

* Proverbs xvii. 14.

to each one of us individually; and the message of God to every human being, written throughout the Scriptures, is "*Thou hast destroyed thyself*, but *in Me*," in me, against whom thou hast sinned, "*is thy help*."*

First.—"*Thou hast destroyed thyself.*" And can there be any doubt of this? God made us for Him-self.† He fashioned our bodies, He breathed into us the breath of life.‡ We belong to Him, body and soul.§ He hath placed us here on trial, and whenever our trial-time is ended, He will send for us, each one at his appointed time, to give an account of his stewardship.‖ Now, what have we done? We all desire to be happy; and God would have us to be so, in love and obedience to Himself, as the great and good God, who is over all, blessed for ever. But, *having no faith in God*, and following our own devices and desires, we are continually trying to find out *for ourselves* what is that good which a man should labour for all the days of his life.¶ And though, from our own bitter experience and that of others, we are learning every day that the world is a *Vanity Fair*, when con-sidered in itself;** and that no real or lasting satis-faction ever has been, or ever can be, in mere worldly things; still we have naturally no faith in

God; we are continually wandering from God's ways, and turning each one of us to his own; we forsake Him, the fountain of living waters, and keep hewing out for ourselves cisterns, broken cisterns which can hold no water.*

The happiness of man is in serving God. And what doth God require of us, but to do justly, to love mercy, and to walk humbly with our God.† Our duty (founded upon our relationship to God and to one another) is, to love our Creator with all the heart, and our neighbour as ourselves; ‡ but there is not upon the earth a just man who doeth good and sinneth not.§ We are *all* verily guilty before God; we are all guilty by our want of faith, by our foolish and wicked wanderings after things hurtful and forbidden,‖ by the things we have done, and by the things we have left undone; by thought, and word, and deed. We are sinful in heart; for out of the heart of man, of *every* man, there naturally proceed evil thoughts.¶ And we are sinful in life; for we have offended God in many things, and have come short in *every* duty.** Iniquity cleaves even to our holy things. God be merciful to *me* a sinner, should be the earnest prayer of every human creature. God is holy and

* Jeremiah ii. 13.   † Micah vi. 8.   ‡ Matt. xxii. 37.   § Eccl. vii. 20.

‖ Isaiah liii. 6.   ¶ Matt. xv. 19.   ** Prov. iii. 20.

hateth sin, whilst we are full of sin. God hath given us a law, holy, just, and good, and hath said, " Cursed is every one who continueth not in all things written in the book of the law to do them,* while we have broken the law, times without number. We have, therefore, earned for ourselves the wages of sin, the curse of God, everlasting separation from God, a home in hell prepared for the devil and his angels.* Thus, according to the testimony of God, confirmed by every man's own conscience, and proved by every man's life, we have destroyed ourselves by the deeds done in the body. And now

> " Compare God's Holiness, God's Justice, and God's Truth
> With wicked, sinful, vile, rebellious man ;
> And see, if thou canst punish sin,
> But let mankind go free."

Secondly.—*In God is our help.* For what was impossible to man's wisdom, and to man's righteousness, the great God, against whom we have so grievously sinned, hath done for us. God hath made a new covenant with man, even the covenant of grace. God, sending His own Son in the likeness of sinful flesh, and for a sin-offering, hath condemned sin in the flesh ; so that the righteousness of the law might be fulfilled in us, who walk not after the flesh but after the Spirit.†

* Gal. vi. 10. Matt. xxv. 41. † Rom. viii. 3.

The Son of God became the Son of man. He, who was the brightness of His Father's glory, and the express image of His person,* was pleased to lay aside the glory which He had with the Father before the world was, and to take upon Him the form of a servant.† He, who was in the beginning with God, and who was God, was made flesh and dwelt among us; and men beheld His glory, the glory as of the only begotten of the Father, full of grace and truth. God was manifest in the flesh. ‡

Jesus (thus named of the angel before he was conceived in the womb) was born at Bethlehem, brought up at Nazareth, and lived chiefly at Capernaum as his own city. When He began to be about thirty years old, He went throughout the cities and villages of Judea preaching and saying, "Repent ye, and believe the gospel." § "And when the Jews inquired of Him, saying, What shall we do, that we may work the works of God? He answered and said, This is the work of God that ye believe in Him whom God hath sent." ‖ Jesus, perfect God and perfect man, in whom dwelt all the fulness of the Godhead bodily, sent to be the great Saviour of men, made Himself in due time a sin-offering for us. He hath once suffered for sins, the just for the unjust.¶ He gave Himself a

* Heb. i. 3. † Phil. ii. 8. ‡ John i. 1—14. § Mark i. 15. ‖ John vi. 28. ¶ 1 Peter iii. 18.

ransom for all.* He became a curse for us to redeem us from the curse of the law.† He fulfilled its righteousness by a perfect obedience, and then paid its awful penalty for transgression. He died for our sins, and rose again for our justification. ‡ In our name and in our nature, He condemned sin in the flesh; so that now, in Christ, God can be just to himself, and yet the justifier of the ungodly.§ In Christ, mercy and truth meet together, righteousness and peace embrace each other. God is in Christ reconciling the world unto Himself, not imputing their trespasses unto them;‖ for Christ, as the Lamb of God, taketh away the sins of the world, having borne the burden in His own body on the accursed tree.¶

Thus, when we had destroyed ourselves, God Himself made a way for our escape, providing for us a Saviour in the person of His own blessed Son, and laying help for us upon one that was mighty to bear. This is a faithful saying, and worthy of all acceptation, that Jesus Christ came into the world to save sinners.** If any man sin, and that is what every man has done, we have an Advocate with the Father, Jesus Christ the righteous, and He is the propitiation for our sins, and not for ours only, but also for the sins of the whole world. † †

---

* 1 Tim. ii. 6. † Gal. iii. 13. ‡ Rom. iv. 25. § Rom. iii. 26. ‖ 2 Cor. v. 19.
¶ John i. 29. 1 Peter ii. 24. ** 1 Tim i. 15. †† 1 John ii. 1.

Thirdly.—Whosoever cometh unto Jesus Christ, confessing his sinfulness with a true heart, and in a childlike spirit—and no man can come unto the Father but by Him*—but "whosoever cometh shall in no wise be cast out ;"† for His blood cleanseth from all sin, and He is able to save to the uttermost.‡ Believe then in the Lord Jesus Christ and thou shalt be saved.§ He that believeth and is baptized shall be saved, and he that believeth not shall be damned.‖ When Jesus Christ had finished the great work which His Father had given Him to do, He commanded His disciples to go into all the world, and preach the gospel to every creature. As your servant for Jesus Christ's sake, I have preached this gospel—these good tidings of great joy—unto you every Sabbath day for above fifteen years; and should I remain with you fifteen years more, Christ Crucified ought to be the centre of my ministerial work; for Christ Crucified is the substance of the Bible, the great subject of the Revelation which God hath made to us; and faith in Christ—not the faith which a man may say he has, but faith which proves itself by good works, by making a man *better* in every relationship of life, and in every particular of his calling—is the work which God requires of every man, whatever his position and whatever his circumstances.

* John xiv. 6. † John vi. 37. ‡ 1 John i. 7. Heb. 7. 25. § Acts xvi. 31. ‖ Mark xvi. 16.

Fourthly.—And now, Who hath believed our report, and to whom hath the arm of the Lord been revealed? Brethren, I thank God, that—amidst many saddening discouragements, and weariness of work, from your unbelief and disobedience to God—there is the great comfort, of having had among us some, to whom to live was Christ and to die gain;* and that others have risen up to fill their places, and are following them as they followed Christ. These are they, to whose hearts the Truth as it is in Jesus has been applied by the power of the Holy Ghost; and who, with the written Word as their rule of life, and the daily grace given in answer to prayer, are fighting the good fight of faith, and seeking to be useful in their day and generation. My dear brethren in Christ, He that conquered *for* you, will conquer *in* you. Ye shall be kept by the power of God through faith;† search the scriptures;‡ enter into your closets, and pray to your Father which seeth in secret; § go up to the courts of the Lord's house; || draw near to the table of the Lord;¶ commune much with your own hearts; ** and have faith in God as your Father in heaven, and He will hold you up by His right hand that your footsteps may not slip. †† He will abide with you always, throughout life and in death: throughout life, for He will enable you, by His Spirit dwelling in you,‡‡

* Phil. i. 21.　† 1 Peter i. 5.　‡ John v. 39.　§ Matt. vi. 6.　|| Neh. x. 25.　¶ Luke xxii. 19.
** Psalm iv. 4.　†† Psalm xvii. 5.　‡‡ John xiv. 60.

to walk worthy of the vocation wherewith ye are called;* to be true men, having an honest heart towards God and your neighbour; to bring forth the fruits of the Spirit—love, joy, peace, gentleness, goodness, faith, meekness, temperance; to occupy faithfully your position; to fulfil rightly your different relationships, to your Queen and country, to your family and the world; and to glorify God at all times and under all circumstances, as the servants of God, till He come: and when your flesh and your strength fail, God will be the strength of your heart and your portion for ever, and you shall have an abundant entrance furnished you into the kingdom of our Lord and Saviour Jesus Christ, for His own name's sake.† The sting of death is sin, and you have grievously sinned; the strength of sin is the law, and by the law you are justly condemned: but, in life and in death, you thank God who has given you the victory through our Lord Jesus Christ.‡ When the work of God, the work of your life, is done in this world; then, having believed on Him whom God hath sent to save you from the guilt and power of sin, you will leave God's service on earth, for God's service in heaven: in the place which Jesus Christ has purchased and prepared for you, you shall have fulness of joy and pleasures for evermore;§ and

*Eph. iv. 1.   † 2 Peter i. 11,   ‡ 1 Cor. xv. 5.   § John xiv. 3.

there at home, for ever with the Lord, I hope to meet you, through the all-sufficient merits of the same blessed Saviour, in whom I put my whole trust. Whilst we live, may we live *for* Him, that when we die, we may die *in* Him. Living or dying, may we be His. He made us for Himself;* He bought us with His blood;† He hath given unto us His Spirit;‡ in Him *only* is our hope;§ but in Him is our *full* confidence,‖ for He never changeth. Whilst in the body, and whilst we have to do with this world, there will ever be a struggle, in our own hearts, between the flesh and the Spirit;¶ and, as we have no sufficiency of ourselves to think or do any good thing, we might well be troubled and afraid; but, strong in the Lord and in the power of His might, we can endure hardness as good soldiers of Jesus Christ,** fighting the good fight of faith, for God Himself will work in us both to will and to do of His good pleasure;†† for if we, being evil, know how to give good gifts to our children, how much more will our Father who is in Heaven, give His Holy Spirit to them that ask Him.‡‡ Strengthened by that Spirit, we can do all things. Have faith, then, in God; pray without ceasing; and the Holy Ghost—the Spirit of Truth— the Comforter—whom the Father will send unto us for Christ's sake, will enable us *to be* and *to do*

* Col. i. 16. † 1 Cor. vi. 20. ‡ 2 Cor. i. 22. § Acts iv. 12. ‖ 2 Tim. i. 12. ¶ Rom. vii. ** Eph. vi. 10. †† Phil. ii. 12. ‡‡ Luke xi. 13.

what God would have us.* The law in our members will ever be warring with the law of our minds; but, by God's help, we shall endure to the end, and be more than conquerors through Him that loved us, crucifying the flesh, renouncing the world, resisting the devil, walking worthy of the vocation wherewith we are called, with all lowliness and meekness, forbearing one another, and forgiving one another, loving our neighbours, and doing good unto all men according to our ability. The great God of heaven is our Father, Jesus Christ is the Captain of our salvation, the Holy Ghost is our guide and our help. Lord God Almighty, we believe in Thee; help thou our unbelief; always and in every thing may be walk by faith and not by sight, till Thou art pleased to send for us into another world.

Fifthly.—But alas! how many of you have neither part nor lot in real, thorough, religion. My heart is very heavy, when I think of your present ungodly state; and the impossibility of your escaping the wrath of God due to your sins, if you continue as you are, neglecting the great salvation which he has provided for you.† You are indeed called Christians, and some of you may perhaps profess to be so; but what then, "Not every one that *saith* unto me,

* John xiv. 26. † Heb. ii. 3.

Lord, Lord, shall enter into the kingdom of heaven, but he that *doeth* the will of my Father which is in heaven.* Are you doing, or even attempting to do the will of God? God has given you the Sabbath to be a sign between you and Him;† but many of you break it nearly as oft as it comes round; for your place in the House of God is almost always empty. God has given you the Bible, that you may prove all things thereby, and hold fast that which is good;‡ but to how many is the Bible a closed book, except when taken down from the shelf, not to learn the truth, and then practise what you learn, but to satisfy your consciences by a little reading. God has said, "Seek ye first the kingdom of God and his righteousness;"§ but these things, if you are even seeking them at all, you are seeking not *first*, but *last*. What shall we eat? what shall we drink? and wherewithal shall we be clothed? are the *great* questions with you, and not how God is to be glorified, and your souls saved. God has made you for himself and for another world, but you have no faith in God, and you are living altogether for what you suppose to be your own interests in this world. Brethren, you are *not* men of God, you know that you are not; you know that you are not even striving to be so: that you are not doing the work of God by a true faith in Him whom God has sent.

* Matt. vii. 21.   † Ezekiel xx. 12.   ‡ 1 John iv. 1.   § Matt vi. 33.

I believe that many of you are much better men than some who make a loud profession, and who appear to be very righteous, by great attention to the externals of religion, whilst their hearts, as proved by their actions, are full of all wickedness and hypocrisy. I believe that some of you, without any profession, are much better men than these; for you are honest and trustworthy, and would scorn a mean action; but I dare not hide it from myself or from you, that you, as well as they, are in the broad path leading to destruction. Broken Sabbaths—the neglected Bible—the worldly-mindedness of the more respectable—the filthy talking, the slanderous words, the common swearing, and the intemperance, &c. of the more hardened—plainly mark you out as those living not for God, but for yourselves. These sins, and such as these, are going before to judgment,* and they will be written against you in the book of God's remembrance.†

Sixthly.—But, brethren, is it always to be thus? Are your hearts so hard, so fast barred against God and against Christ, that you are determined to keep Him waiting, and not open them unto Him, though He has stood knocking at the door for so many years?‡ By the mercies of God, and by the value

* 1 Tim. v. 24.   † Rev. xx. 12.   ‡ Rev. iii. 20.

of your immortal souls, stop and think before it be quite too late. God's Spirit will not always strive with man.* The day of grace may be ended before the day of life. God may say of you, even now, " Let them alone."† " I have called, but ye refused ; I have stretched out my hand, and no man regarded : but ye have set at nought all my counsel, and would none of my reproof; I also will mock at your calamity, I will mock when your fear cometh; when your fear cometh as a desolation, and your destruction cometh as a whirlwind, when distress and anguish cometh upon you."‡ God cannot be mocked ; whatsoever a man soweth, that shall he also reap; if he sow to the flesh, he shall of the flesh reap corruption; if he sow to the Spirit, he shall of the Spirit reap life everlasting. § In this world you never expect a good harvest when you have neglected seed-time, or when you have sown bad seed in a poor soil ; so, for the next world, you will reap as you sow. There will be a great gulf, which no man can pass,‖ between those who serve God and those who serve Him not.¶ How can ye be amongst the children of God *then*, when you are not amongst them *now?* I beseech you, in Christ's stead, be ye reconciled to God. Seek ye the Lord *while* He may be found, and call ye upon Him *while* He is near.**

* Gen. vi. 3.   † Hosea vi. 17.   ‡ Proverbs i. 24.   § Gal. vi. 7.   ‖ Luke xvi. 26.
¶ Malachi iii. 18.   ** Isaiah lv. vi.

During our Relationship, I have had to bury all the old inhabitants of the parish, with but two or three exceptions. They have gone the way of all flesh, and many of the young and the middle-aged are sleeping with them, as to the body, in our Church yard. The sun shines, the birds sing, the world goes on as usual; and their places are filled up. Many, who were children 15 years ago, have been married, and are now heads of houses. They too, at the end of every day, are a day's march nearer home, and will have to go hence very soon. Such is our life on earth. We are not to live here always, and if it be with us, as it ought to be, we would not wish to live always in this world. But when we leave it, taking nothing, as we brought nothing, what then? yea, what then? This surely is the great question, above all other questions, for every one of us. Better or worse, richer or poorer, we shall have done with this world before long, and what then? yea, what then? If you have done God's work; if, living and dying, you have been in God's service on earth; then, for the sake of Jesus Christ, you will have to do God's work, and live in God's service for ever in heaven; and what must it be to be there! But, if you have done your own work, and lived for your own interests, then, as it was with the angels who kept not their first estate, so will it be with you; their place will be yours;* a place of outer darkness, where there will be weeping, and wailing, and gnashing of teeth, where the worm dieth not, and the fire is not quenched.† Ye knew your duty, but ye did it not; willingly and wilfully ye refused to do God's work, yielding to the unbelief of your own hearts, and the temptations of the world and the devil; and far, far better had you never been born,‡ if you turn not to the Lord, that He may have mercy upon you, and to our God that He may abundantly pardon, while there is time.

I know that in my own work of caring for your souls, I have greatly failed; and that I need the atonement of Christ for my ministerial shortcomings, as well as for my personal transgressions; but, brethren, I have striven, in some measure, to fulfil the duties of our relationship. In the Church and at your own houses, in the fields and by the wayside, I have endeavoured, however feebly, to labour among you as the servant of God, and your servant for Jesus Christ's sake. Fifteen years of the best part of my life have been spent in your service; though, as regards very many of you, I have laboured in vain, and spent my strength for nought. God knoweth that I have kept back nothing which I thought profitable to you, either for this world

* Matt. xxv. 41. † Mark ix. 44. ‡ Matt. xxvi. 24.

or the next; and that I would not shrink from any thing that might be for your good. Pray for me, that God, by His Spirit, would make me more diligent in His work, and more faithful in my relationship to you. Pray for yourselves—and never shall I cease to pray for you—that by the same Holy Spirit, God would revive His work in the midst of us, making you *individually* the servants of God, and making us, as *a parish*, diligent and prosperous in every good thing, striving together for the furtherance of the Gospel. May this written letter help us, under God, in our Relationship and in our Work.

I have written at greater length, as it is my first letter to you—will doubtless be my last—and may perhaps be read by some of you, from time to time, during my life and after my death. But that I may not be too wearisome, I must now conclude.

I can only pray that *every man* in this Parish of Hoole, may so live whilst on earth, that *every man* may be found perfect in the day of the Lord Jesus.* It is now Easter when I am writing these last words, and I intend (God willing) to give every householder a printed copy at Whitsuntide. Might I ask, that, both when you read it, and at other

* Col. i. 28.

times, you would pray for yourselves and your Minister, that the glorious *Facts* which, at such seasons, are had in special remembrance, may be continually in our minds, and that the great *Doctrines* founded on these facts, may have their due influence, by the power of the Holy Ghost, continually on our hearts. Then, when Christ comes to judge the quick and dead, our dead bodies being raised from the grave, and fashioned like unto Christ's glorious body, we shall, with soul and body re-united, be for ever with the Lord,* delighting to do His will and perform His pleasure, even as the angels of Heaven. Amen, and Amen.†

" Prepare to meet thy God.

Death and judgment are at hand: heaven or hell will be thy home.

Jesus, who is coming to judge, now waits to save.
Believe: Love."

The peace of God which passeth all understanding, keep your hearts and minds in the knowledge and love of God, and of His Son, Jesus Christ our Lord: and the blessing of God Almighty—the Father, the Son, and the Holy Ghost—be upon you, and remain with you always.

I am, my dear Parishioners,
Your Servant in Jesus Christ,

Easter, 1864. ROBERT BRICKEL.

* 1 Thess. iv. 17. † Psalm ciii. 21.

OMISSION, 33RD PAGE, 8TH LINE.

God has commanded us to make prayers and supplications for all men—for enemies, as well as friends—for the Jew and the Heathen, as well as for our immediate neighbours. To those, amongst whom we live, we can always be doing good in many ways, according to the blessing, wherewith God has blessed us; whilst, by the different societies, established for this purpose, we can send help to the uttermost parts of the earth, that God's Kingdom may come, and God's Will be done in Earth as it is in Heaven.

www.ingramcontent.com/pod-product-compliance
Lightning Source LLC
Chambersburg PA
CBHW081304040426
42452CB00014B/2647